Panorama

FOTOGRAFIEN VON / PHOTOGRAPHED BY
DALIBOR KUSÁK

TEXT VON / WRITTEN BY
LYDIA PETRÁŇOVÁ

50
Bilder Pictures
aus Böhmen from Bohemia
und Mähren and Moravia

PANORAMA
PRAG / PRAGUE

Umschlag Vorderseite: Burg Karlstein
Umschlag Rückseite: Beskiden

Front cover: Karlštejn Castle
Back cover: The Beskydy mountains

ISBN 80-7038-243-0

Immer wieder wird einfach gesagt, Böhmen und Mähren lägen im Herzen oder auch in der Mitte Europas. Ganz richtig ist das wohl nicht. Ein Blick auf die Karte zeigt, daß diese Länder ein paar hundert Kilometer westlich von einem Idealschnittpunkt der Längen- und Breitengrade liegen, die Europa in der Nordsüd- und Ostwestrichtung halbieren, und deshalb eigentlich zu Westeuropa gehören müßten. Stattdessen bezeichnen viele zeitgenössische Publizisten und Politiker, von der über 40 Jahre anhaltenden Orientierung der Tschechoslowakei auf dem mächtigen Nachbarn im Osten bestimmt, diese Länder als osteuropäisch. So sind also geographische und politische Kriterien durcheinandergeraten und die Frage bleibt, wann es gelingt, die Dinge wieder auf den rechten Stand zu bringen.

In der Mitte Europas liegen Böhmen und Mähren nun zweifellos, wenn man diese Mitte als einen Schnittpunkt lebenswichtiger Funktionen im Sinn hat (Schließlich nimmt das Herz im menschlichen Körper auch keine ideale Zentrallage ein). Hier entspringen Flüsse, die zu den verschiedenen, die Küsten Europas in allen Himmelsrichtungen umspülenden Meeren fließen, hier schneiden sich die wichtigsten europäischen Verbindungswege zu Land und in der Luft. Genau so überschneiden und durchdringen einander hier die verschiedensten Strömungen menschlicher Kultur.

Die zahlreiche Spuren einer prähistorischen Besiedlung werden von den Archäologen untersucht. Die bedeutsamen Entdeckungen von Siedlungen paläolithischer Mammutjäger, die sich vor 28 tausend Jahren bei den Pavlov-Hügeln in Südmähren niedergelassen hatten, hat einer der vorzeitlichen Kulturen in der internationalen Archäologische-Fachsprache die Bezeichnung „Pavlovien" eingetragen. Über lange Zeiträume hinweg haben Jäger, Hirten und Ackerbauern aus den veschiedenen Kulturen an geeigneten Stellen ihre Heimstätten errichtet. In den Jahrhunderten unmittelbar vor dem Eintreffen der Slawen wurde dies Land von Kelten und Germanen bebaut, die bereits Eisenwerkzeuge und -waffen benutzten. In Südmähren hielten sich sogar die Römer auf, die hier im 2. Jahrhundert n. Chr. bei Musov ihre vordersten Befestigungen nördlich der Donau hinterlassen haben. Slawische Stämme begannen sich gegen Ende des 5. Jahrhunderts n. Chr. in Böhmen und Mähren niederzulassen. Der Nationalmythos weiß von einem Urvater des Tschechenstamms namens Čech zu berichten, der seine Scharen in die Tiefebene am Zusammenfluß von Moldau und Elbe geführt haben soll, zweier Flüsse, die als Lebensadern des Böhmerlandes gelten müssen. Er erstieg den Berg Říp und der Ausblick auf das umliegende fruchtbare Land ergriff ihn so, daß er beschloß, sich mit seinem Volke auf immer hier anzusiedeln. Die Bewohner Böhmens und Mährens, die tschechische Sprache und einige ihrer immer noch lebendigen Dialekte sprechend, stellen heute die am weitesten westlich lebenden Slawen dar.

Die Slawen betrieben Ackerbau, Viehzucht und verehrten als Gottheiten Naturkräfte, wobei sie sich mit magischen Ritualen des Erfolgs für ihr Tun zu versichern suchten. Dem Christentum begegneten sie erst im 9. Jahrhundert. Einer mittelalterlichen Chronik zufolge haben 845 zu Regensburg vierzehn tschechische Edle die Taufe angenommen. Im Jahre 863 trafen die Slawenapostel Konstans und Methodius aus Byzanz in Mähren ein, von Fürst Svatopluk aus der Mojmiriden-Dynastie gerufen. Der war

Herrscher des großmährischen Reichs, dem auch die in Böhmen, der Westslowakei und den umliegenden Landen lebenden slawischen Stämme untertan waren. Nachdem nun das großmährische Reich mit Beginn des 10. Jahrhunderts untergegangen war, verlagerten sich die Einigungsbestrebungen der Slawenstämme nach Böhmen.

Hier gewannen die Fürsten aus dem Geschlecht der Přemysliden die Oberhand und erweiterten allmählich ihren Einfluß, bis sie schließlich ganz Böhmen und Mähren unter ihre Botmäßigkeit gebracht hatten. Schon um 885 besetzte der Přemyslidenfürst Bořivoj einen Felsrücken über der Moldau, eine Kultstätte, an der seit jeher die freien Stammesangehörigen ihr Thing hielten und ihren gewählten Fürsten auf einen steinernen Thron erhoben. Bořivoj hat diese heilige Stätte befestigt und hier die Burg Prag angelegt. Seither, also eigentlich schon seit dem 11. Jahrhundert, wird von hier aus der tschechische Staat regiert. Allein von daher nimmt Prag unter den Hauptstädten der übrigen europäischen Ländern eine ganz einzigartige Stellung ein.

Die um eine Festigung des tschechischen Staats verdienten Přemysliden verblieben an dessen Spitze bis 1306, erst als Fürsten, nach dem Erlaß der Goldenen Bulle durch den römischen Kaiser 1212 als erbliche Könige. Der Beginn ihrer Herrschaft war von grausamem Ehrgeiz und brudermörderischem Zwist gekennzeichnet, wie das auch in den übrigen europäischen Dynastien gang und gäbe war. Ihre Herkunft leiteten die Přemysliden aus dem Ehebund des mythischen Ackermanns Přemysl und der mit seherischen Kräften begabten Fürstin Libuše ab. Ihren Einfluß stützten sie auf den Kult der ältesten tschechischen Heiligen, vor allem auf den St. Wenzelskult, eines Fürsten aus dem Přemyslidenhaus, den die Geschichte in die europäische Galerie der sog. heiligen Herrscher neben Karl den Großen, Ludwig den

Heiligen, Stephan von Ungarn u. a. eingereiht hat. Um das Jahr 973 wurde das Prager Bistum gegründet, 1063 das Bistum Olmütz.

Im Rahmen des Přemyslidenstaats kam Mähren, das als fürstliches Lehen und Markgrafschaft von Verwandten des Herrschers auf den Burgen Olmütz, Brünn und Znajm regiert wurde, eine Sonderstellung zu.

Um eine Ausdehnung der urbaren Fläche, Verbreitung von Bildung und Entwicklung des Gold- und Silbererzbergbaus haben sich in hohem Maß Klöster verdient gemacht, die von den Herrschern seit Ende des 10. Jahrhunderts mit Fleiß gegründet und anfänglich mit dem Benediktiner-, später dem Zisterzienser- und Prämonstratenserorden beschickt wurden. Eine Hochblüte erlebte der tschechische Staat insbesondere im 13. Jahrhundert, als unter dem Einfluß günstiger Klimabedingungen, neuer Ackerbauverfahren und dem Gewinn aus der Edelmetallschürferei viele neue Dörfer entstanden und befestigte Städte mit spezialisierten Handwerkern aus dem Boden wuchsen. Die Einwohnerzahlen kletterten teils durch natürlichen Zuwachs, teils durch den Zuzug vieler Kolonisten aus westlichen Ländern, hauptsächlich aus den Rheinlanden. Jahrhundertelang lebten so tschechisch- und deutschsprachige Bewohner Böhmens und Mährens ohne größere Probleme miteinander, praktisch bis zum Aufkommen des modernen Nationalismus.

Mit der Blüte des Königreichs stieg auch das Prestige des böhmischen Königs. Přemysl Otakar II. (1253–1278) wurde seines Reichtums und seiner Macht halber der „eiserne und goldene" König genannt. Er konnte sich auf ein Netz aus starken Burgen (z. B. Bezděz/Bösig, Zvíkov/Klingenberg, Písek) stützen, durch Eroberungen und gewandte Politik sein Staatsgebiet erweitern und reckte sogar die Hand nach der Kaiserkrone aus. Seine persönlichen Ambitionen hat er in der Schlacht auf dem

Marchfeld mit dem Leben bezahlt, doch ist das Prestige des böhmischen Königreichs in Mitteleuropa weiter gestiegen. Přemysls Sohn Wenzel II. war gleichzeitig auch König von Polen und gewann für seinen Sohn Wenzel III. die ungarische Krone hinzu. Als durch die Ermordung Wenzels III. die Přemysliden männlicherseits ausgestorben waren, stellte der böhmische Staat das mächtigste Staatsgebilde in Mitteleuropa dar. Er besaß ein Netz von strategisch bedeutenden Burgen und befestigten Städten, ertragreiche Silbergruben in Iglau und Kuttenberg sowie eine hochwertige Münze, den seit 1300 geprägten sog. Prager Groschen.

Mit der Vermählung der Přemyslidenprinzessin Elisabeth und des Prinzen Johann von Luxemburg (1310–1346 König) begann die Ära der Luxemburgerdynastie. Am nachhaltigsten griff Karl IV. (1346–1378), böhmischer und römischer König, seit 1355 auch römischer Kaiser, in die europäische Politik ein. Er war am französischen Hof aufgewachsen und hatte eine für seine Zeit außerordentliche Bildung erlangt. Karl zeigte diplomatisches Talent und politische Weitsicht, indem er die Geschicke des böhmischen Königreichs mit der Zukunft des Hauses Luxemburg verband. Er knüpfte ans Přemyslidenerbe an und festigte die Macht des Herrschers in seinem Länderbund, der als Lande der böhmischen Krone bezeichnet wurde. Als sichtbare Insignie dieser Macht ließ er eine überaus kostbare Köngskrone anfertigen, die zugleich auch ein heiliges Reliquienbehältnis war. Diese wird heute in einem besonderen Tresor im Veitsdom auf dem Hradschin aufbewahrt.

Die Lande der böhmischen Krone baute Karl mit Bedacht zu einer Grundlage der kaiserlichen Hausmacht aus und machte Prag zur Reichshauptstadt. Er erweitere es um die großzügig entworfene Neustadt, ließ das Prager Bistum zum Erzbistum erheben, gründete hier die erste mitteleuropäische Universität (1348) und entwickelte durch die Förderung der Bauhütte Peter Parlers eine grandiose Bautätigkeit. Aus jener Zeit besitzt Prag gotische Kleinodien wie z. B. den Veitsdom und die Karlsbrücke. Als sicheren Hort für die Kroninsignien Böhmens und des Reichs ließ Karl IV. die Burg Karlstein bauen, die berühmteste der böhmischen Burgen. Er förderte Gelehrsamkeit und Künste, diplomatischen Mitteln gab er den Vorzug vor Waffengewalt.

Als ein Ort der Gelehrsamkeit leistete Prag seinen Beitrag zur europäischen Reformation. Auf Beschluß des Konstanzer Konzils wurden zwei tschechische Reformatoren zu Ketzern erklärt und auf den Scheiterhaufen geschickt, die Magister Johannes Hus (1415) und Hieronymus von Prag (1416). Die Lehre dieser Reformatoren war in breiten Volksschichten ausgesprochen populär geworden. Zum Symbol der Husanhänger – der Hussiten – wurde der Kelch als Zeichen für das Abendmahl in beiderlei Gestalt. 1420 gründeten die Hussiten in Südböhmen die Stadt Tábor, von wo aus unter der Führung ihrer Hauptleute, vor allem unter dem Heerführer Jan Žižka, ihre Heerhaufen gegen die „Widersacher des Kelchs" ins Feld zogen. In den Jahren 1420–1431 setzten sich die Hussiten erfolgreich gegen fünf Kreuzzüge zur Wehr, zu denen der Heilige Stuhl wider die böhmischen Ketzer aufgerufen hatte. Die Kriege der Hussiten gegen auswärtige Feinde und einheimische katholische Adelige dauerten lange Jahren und richteten im Land immense Verwüstungen an, doch konnten die Hussiten ihre Reformation behaupten.

So wurde König Georg von Podiebrad (1458––1471 zum Herrscher über zweierlei Volk: über Katholiken und Reformierte. Die diplomatische Gesandtschaft, die dieser König an die Herrscher der europäischen Länder mit seinen Vorschlägen zu einem Friedensbündnis gegen die Türkengefahr ausgeschickt hatte, sollte schließlich bis ans äußerste Ende der damals bekannten Welt gelangen, bis zum Kap Finisterre. In seinen vom Krieg heimgesuchten Ländern stellte König Georg die Ordnung wieder her, auch Handwerk und Bergbau erlebten eine neue Blüte. Die Auswirkungen diese Konjunktur sollten sich aber erst unter seinen Nachfolgern, den Herrschern aus der Jagellonendynastie zeigen. Im Stil der Spätgotik wurde damals auf der Prager Burg, auf Křivoklát (Pürglitz) und in Kuttenberg gebaut.

Mit dem einsetzenden 16. Jahrhundert kam allmählich – allerdings mit einiger Verspätung – die Renaissance zum Durchbruch, vornehmlich bei Umbauten von Burgen zu Schlössern sowie bei Schloßneubauten. Bauherren waren die Aristokraten, denen zu jener Zeit ihre Großgutbewirtschaftung beträchtliche Einkünfte aus neu angelegten Fischteichen, Mühlen und Brauereien zufließen ließ. In Südböhmen waren das die Rosenberger (Český Krumlov/Krumau), in Ostböhmen die Pernsteiner (Litomyšl), aber auch andere Adelshäuser. Das 16. Jahrhundert war eine Blütezeit für Handwerk und Handel, und so erfuhren auch Bürgerhäuser Renaissanceumbauten, bei denen Interieur und Fassade verwandelt wurden. In manchen Städten sind zusammenhängende Renaissancehäuserzeilen bis auf den heutigen Tag erhalten, z. B. in Telč, Slavonice (Zlabings) oder Nové Město n. Metují (Neustadt an der Mettau).

Ab 1526 waren Böhmen und Mähren Bestandteil der mitteleuropäischen Vielvölkermonarchie unter den österreichischen Habsburgern. Die zentralen Reichsbehörden und Herrscher siedelten mit Ausnahme der rudolphinischen Ära in Wien. Kaiser Rudolph II. (1576–1612) verlegte seine Residenz nach Prag und hat so dessen Bedeutung als politische Metropole des Reichs wieder aufleben lassen. Prag wurde von diplomatischen Gesandtschaften aufgesucht und dank der persönlichen kaiserlichen Liebhabereien auch von namhaften Künstlern und Gelehrten jener Zeit, insbesondere von Astronomen (J. Kepler, Tycho de Brahe) und Alchymisten.

Zwischen dem katholischen Herrscher, bestrebt, alle Macht in die eigenen Hände zu konzentrieren, und den böhmischen Ständen (Adel und Städtevertretungen) nahmen die Mißhelligkeiten zu, um dann 1618 zu kulminieren, als Vertreter von oppositionellem Adel und Bürgerschaft die königlichen Statthalter im wahrsten Sinne des Wortes aus einem Fenster der Prager Burg stürzten. Anschließend erfolgte die Kürung des Kurfürsten Friedrich von der Pfalz zum König, woraufhin der als Böhmischer Krieg bezeichnete bewaffnete Konflikt ausbrach, der eigentlich Auftakt zu einer wesentlich umfangreicheren Auseinandersetzung werden sollte – zum Dreißigjährigen Krieg. In der ersten Etappe, im Böhmischen Krieg, siegten die Habsburger. Friedrichs Heer unterlag 1620 in der Schlacht auf dem Weißen Berg unweit von Prag und Kaiser Ferdinand II. demonstrierte 1621 seinen Sieg mit der Hinrichtung von 27 führenden böhmischen Politikern auf dem Altstädter Ring. In den folgenden Jahren, als der Krieg dann auf einen Großteil des europäischen Territoriums übergriff, sollte der ehrgeizige General Albrecht von Wallenstein auf den mitteleuropäischen Schlachtfeldern eine bedeutende Rolle spielen, um schließlich auf kaiserliches Geheiß 1634 in Cheb (Eger) ermordet zu werden. Kaum einer Gestalt haben Geschichtsschreibung und Belletristik so viel Aufmerksamkeit zukommen lassen wie gerade diesem kriegerischen Abenteurer und Parvenü sowie seinem mutmaßlichen Verrat.

Nach der Niederlage der böhmischen Stände schlug der Kaiser gegenüber den Ländern der böhmische Krone einen harten Rekatholisierungskurs ein und viele Personen evangelischer Konfession mußten ins Exil gehen. Unter ihnen auch der bedeutende Philosoph und Pädagoge J. A. Comenius.

Der Nachkriegs-Bauboom in der zweiten Hälfte des 17. und der ersten Hälfte des 18. Jahrhunderts stand schon gänzlich im Zeichen des Barockstils. Am Bau der Barockdome, -schlösser und -paläste arbeiteten führende europäische Baumeister wie C. Lurago, K. I. Dientzenhofer, J. B. Santini und andere. Ihre Bauwerke wurden von den Schöpfungen barocker Bildhauer und Maler (z. B. F. M. Brokof, P. Brandl) geziert, die bis heute Bewunderung finden. Einzigartige barocke „Freiluft-Galerien" sind die Karlsbrücke und die Skulpturen von M. B. Braun in Kuks. Die Schloßinterieurs erfüllten das aristokratischen Verlangen nach Luxus und Bequemlichkeit, aber auch nach Unterhaltung. Die Säle, Theater, Musiksalons und Kapellen der Schlösser waren Stätten einer Musik, die im Verein mit den musizierenden Kantoren und kirchlichen Laienmusikanten die tschechische Musiktradition aufkommen ließen. Dank dieser Tradition konnte sich schon W. A. Mozart in Prag recht verstanden fühlen. Später, zur Zeit der bürgerlichen Gesellschaft, entwuchsen ihr Musiker von Weltruhm wie B. Smetana, A. Dvořák, L. Janáček, B. Martinů und andere.

Die Industrialisierung nahm in Böhmen einen geringfügig schnelleren Verlauf als in den übrigen Ländern des Habsburger Staatengebildes. Hand in Hand mit der Erstarkung des tschechischen Kapitals meldeten sich auch Bestrebung um nationale Emanzipation und staatsrechtlichen Ausgleich. Die neuzeitliche tschechische Gesellschaft hat sich zunächst in der ersten Hälfte des 19. Jahrhunderts kulturell, in der zweiten Hälfte auch politisch formiert und der starre Panzer der Habsburger Monarchie wurde ihr allmählich zu eng. An der Schwelle des 1. Weltkriegs waren Böhmen und Mähren zu den höchstindustrialisierten Ländern der Donaumonarchie geworden, leider auch zu ihrer Waffenschmiede. Aus der Rüstungsfabriken der Industriestädte wie Pilsen oder Brünn stammte die an der Front Tod und Verderben speiende Munition. Viele tschechische Soldaten weigerten sich, für die Interessen des Habsburgerreichs zu kämpfen und liefen zu den Legionen auf Seiten der Entente über. Zusammen mit den Exilpolitikern mit Tomáš G. Masaryk an der Spitze haben diese Legionäre ihren Beitrag dazu geleistet, daß in der Nachkriegsordnung Europas als einer der Nachfolgerstaaten der alten Habsburgermonarchie die unabhängige Tschechoslowakei entstehen konnte. Im Jahr 1969 wurde dieser Staat zu einer Föderation aus zwei Republiken umgeformt, wobei die Tschechische Republik die historischen böhmischen Kronländer, also Böhmen, Mähren und einen Teil Schlesiens einschließt.

Bei einer Beschreibung der böhmischen Lande haben schon die Geographen des 17. Jahrhunderts den Umstand betont, daß diese nach allen Seiten von Gebirgen mit undurchdringlichen Wäldern gesäumt seien, die einen natürlichen Grenzwall gegen Feinde darstellten. Die böhmische Höhenzüge sind keine Hochgebirge (der höchste Berg, die Schneekoppe im Riesengebirge, ist 1602 m hoch) und sind im Lauf der Erdzeitalter abgetragen und abgerundet worden, einige wenige Gebiete jüngeren vulkanischen Ursprungs ausgenommen, vor allem das Böhmische Mittelgebirge. Gut markierte Wanderwege ermöglichen hier gefahrlose Touren. Einige Berge sind zu Nationalsymbolen geworden und leben von alters her in den Mythen: Říp (St. Georgsberg), Blaník, Radhošť. Der Große Schneeberg (Kralický Sněžník) wird auch das Dach Europas genannt, da er die Wasserscheide zu Ostsee, Nordsee und dem Schwarzen Meer darstellt.

Bergfreunde klettern mit unterschiedlicher Risokofreude und Abenteuerlust in den Felsen umher, die in Ost- und Nordböhmen als ganze Felsstädte mit bizzarren Gebilden (Pravčicer Tor) auftreten, andere seilen sich in die

Schluchten und Höhlen der Karstgebiete ab. Die Elisabethenhöhle im bekannten Mährischen Karst hat wohl als erste Höhle der Welt eine elektrische Beleuchtung bekommen (1880). Die Vorstellung von einer natürlichen Grenzbefestigung durch tiefe, dichte Wälder kann im Kernwaffenzeitalter nur noch ein wehmütiges Lächeln hervorlocken, doch stellt jener bewaldete Gebirgskranz einen beträchtlichen Schatz für das Land dar. Hier liegen die meisten Naturschutzgebiete (Nationalpark Riesengebirge, einige Dutzend Reservationen und Schutzgebiete), die fast 14 % Fläche der Tschechischen Republik ausmachen. Der Naturschutz kann in diesem Land auf eine alte Tradition zurückblicken. Als erstes Gelände wurde der in Südböhmen befindliche Sophien-Urwald (Žofínský prales) 1838 zum Naturschutzgebiet erklärt. Als überhaupt eine der ersten sah die Verfassung dieses Staats auch eine Naturschutzregelung vor, doch hat die stürmische Industrialisierung das Gesetz vielfach mißachtet. Vor allem in Nordwestböhmen und im Ostrauer Gebiet ist die Natur heute im wahrsten Sinne des Wortes schwerkrank und eine Gesundung wird ungeheure Anstrengungen kosten. Naturschutz ist heute eine professionelle Angelegenheit, daneben sind aber auch tausende von freiwilligen Naturschützern, Liebhaber-Ornithologen, Weidmännern und Fischern am Werk. Gefährdete und exotische Tierarten werden in den zoologischen Gärten gehalten, deren Netz in Böhmen das dichteste der Welt ist (15 Zoos).

Seit Jahrhunderten wurden hier Bodenschätze abgebaut: Schon im Mittelalter wurden die goldführenden Sande der Otava (Wotau) ausgesiebt, die Goldschächte von Jílové (Eylau) bei Prag und die Silberminen von Jihlava (Iglau) und Kutná Hora (Kuttenberg)

erschöpft. Der Uranbergbau in Jáchymov (Joachimstal) ist zu Ende gegangen, die Kohlenflöze werden knapper. Unvermindert fließen aber immer noch die wohltuenden Mineralquellen. Die berühmtesten der 34 böhmischen Heilbäder konzentrieren sich auf Nordwest- und Westböhmen. Eine Liste der Besucher, die allein in Karlsbad (Karlovy Vary) und Marienbad (Mariánské Lázně) der Kur und Geselligkeit halber geweilt haben, würde zu einer Aufzählung aller, die Rang und Namen in der europäischen Kultur und Politik und/oder ein entsprechendes Vermögen ihr eigen nannten. Zum Weltruf von Karlsbad haben auch die dortigen Internationalen Filmfestspiele beigetragen.

Böhmen und Mähren sind reich gegliederte und unendlich vielgestaltige Landstriche. Nicht nur von der Natur geformt oder in den von Menschenhand geprägten Agrar- und Industrielandschaften, sonden auch durch ihre kulturellen Spezifika wie die regionalen Volksarchitekturen, Mundarten, traditionellen Handarbeiten aus Keramik, Holz und Textil sowie die lebende Folklore. An traditionsverhafteter Folklore war Mähren immer der reichere Landesteil, vor allem sein Osten, in dem man bis auf den heutigen Tag Festtrachten, traditionell verzierten Bauten und einem lautstark-fröhlich Brauchtum im Jahresablauf begegnet. (Fasching, Königsreiten usw.). In Strážnice, wo sich auch ein wichtiges Freilichtmuseum, das Museum des südostmährischen Dorfs befindet, werden alljährlich bekannte Internationale Folklorefestivals abgehalten.

Nur schwerlich läßt sich beschreiben, was ein Betrachter empfinden muß. Etwa die Atmosphäre der südböhmischen Moorlanddörfer mit den farbenfrohen Hausgiebeln im Stil des Bauernbarock mit Nebelschleiern über den umlie-

genden Wiesen und spiegelblanken Wasserflä-
chen der großen Teiche. Die Atmosphäre einer
Landschaft, die der Dichter ein „versonnenes
Land" nennt. Oder hingegen die Unruhe und
Faszination inmitten der bizarren Höhen des
windumtosten Böhmischen Mittelgebirges, die
Harmonie im Werk von Natur und Mensch in
einer Landschaft, die Böhmisches Paradies
genannt wird, die Jahrhunderte überdauernde
Reglosigkeit des Böhmerwalds, die pfahlge-
spickten Weinberge unter der sengenden südmährischen Sonne oder die Kakofonie der
Schafglocken im walachischen Beskidenvorland.

Nicht zufällig ist das Lied Kde domov můj
(Wo ist mein Heim) aus dem Jahr 1834, aus der
Zeit der tschechischen nationalen Wiederge-
burt, als die neuzeitliche tschechische Nation
schwer um ihre Identität ringen mußte, zur
Hymne dieses Landes geworden. In diesem
Lied wird anders als in anderen Hymnen nicht
von Stärke und Macht gesungen, sondern von
strömenden Flüssen, rauschenden Wäldern und
blühenden Gärten. Es ist nicht leicht, im Herzen Europas zu leben, in das von jeher auch die
Usurpatoren und Eroberer an der Spitze ihrer
Armeen ihre Schritte lenkten. Nicht viele Länder dieser Ende sind so mit Mahnmalen der
Gewalt und des sinnlosen Todes übersät wie die
böhmischen und mährischen Lande. Zerstreut
zwischen jenen Auen, Wäldern und Feldern,
wollen sie den künftigen Generationen ein
Memento sein.

FROM THE HISTORY OF BOHEMIA AND MORAVIA

It is generally stated that Bohemia and Moravia
lie in the heart, or also the centre, of Europe.
That's not entirely true. A glance at the map will
show you that they lie a good few hundred kilometres west of the exact longitude-latitude intersection of Europe, so that they should belong
to western Europe. On the other hand, many
present-day publicists and politicians, influen-
ced by the more than forty years of Czechoslovakia's political orientation towards its power-
ful eastern neighbour, call it an east European
country. So geographical criteria have got
mixed up with political ones, and who knows
when things will get straightened out.

But Bohemia and Moravia do undoubtedly
lie in the centre of Europe if you think of the
centre as the intersection of vitally important
functions. (Anyway the human heart does not
take a central position in the body either). From
here rivers run to the seas that surround Europe
from all points of the compass, the main European lines of communication cross here, both
on land and in the air. And so too the most
diverse trends of human culture have crossed
and intertwined here for many thousands of
years.

Archeologists are studying numerous traces
of prehistoric settlements. One ancient culture
has been given the name "pavlovien" in international archeological terminology from important discoveries of paleolithic settlements of
mammoth hunters in the Pavlov hills in southern Moravia 28 thousand years ago. Hunters,
shepherds and farmers of various cultures have
built their homes in suitable places through the
ages. During the centuries preceding the arrival
of the Slavs the land here was cultivated by Celts
and Teutons, who used iron tools and weapons.
Romans too lived in south Moravia, and left

there their most northerly fortified ramparts on the Danube near Mušov in the second century A. D. Slav tribes began to settle in Bohemia and Moravia towards the end of the fifth century A. D. A national legend tells how the forefather of the tribe of Čechs (or Czechs), whose name was Čech, led his company to the lowlands around the confluence of the Vltava and the Elbe, rivers that are the arteries of the Czech lands. He climbed the little hill called Říp, and was so enchanted by the view of the surrounding fertile country that he decided to settle there with his people for ever. The inhabitants of Bohemia and Moravia, speaking the Czech language and several still living dialects of it, are today the westernmost Slavs.

The Slavs ploughed the soil, kept cattle and called on the forces of nature in magic rituals to ensure them success. They met Christianity only in the ninth century. A medieval chronicle records that in 845 in Regensburg fourteen Bohemian princes had themselves christened. In 863 the Slav missionaries Cyril and Methodius came to Moravia from Byzantium. They were invited by Prince Svatopluk, of the House of Mojmír, ruler of the Great Moravian Empire, to whom the Slav tribes living in Bohemia, western Slovakia and adjoining territories were subjected. When the Moravian Empire was destroyed at the beginning of the tenth century, attempts to unite the Slav tribes were transferred to Bohemia.

Here the princes of the House of Přemyslides gained superiority over the others and gradually their influence spread to cover the whole of Bohemia and Moravia. Around 885 the Přemyslide prince Bořivoj occupied the rocky headland over the Vltava, a cult site where since time immemorial the free members of the tribe had held assemblies and installed their elected prince upon a stone throne. Bořivoj fortified this sacred place and built on it a castle called Praha (Prague). Since then, that is for eleven centuries, the Bohemian state has been administered from there. This fact gives Prague a unique position among the capitals of Europe.

The Přemyslides, thanks to whom the Czech state was unified, remained at its head till 1306, first as princes and then, after the Roman Emperor issued the Sicilian Golden Bull in 1212, as hereditary kings. The beginnings of their rule was marked by cruel ambition and fratricidal quarrels, like the beginnings of other European dynasties. The Přemyslides are said to have originated from the union between the mythical farmer, Přemysl the Ploughman, and the Princess Libuše, who had the gift of prophesy. Their influence was based on the cult of the oldest Bohemian saints, in the first place St. Václav (Wenceslas), a prince of the House of Přemyslides, whom history includes in the European gallery of "holy sovereigns" beside Charlemagne, Louis the Great, Stephan of Hungary and others. Around 973 a bishopric was founded in Prague, in 1063 in Olomouc.

Right from the beginning Moravia held a special position in the Přemyslide state, and was administered by relatives of the king as a feudal benefice and margravedom from castles in Olomouc, Brno and Znojmo.

It was to a great extent thanks to the monasteries, which the kings diligently established from the end of the tenth century for the monks of, first, the Benedictine and, later, the Cistercian and Premonstratensian orders, that cultivated areas of land were enlarged, education spread, the mining of precious metals developed and technical novelties widely used. The Bohemian state flourished particularly in the 13th century when, owing to favourable climatic conditions, the use of new farming methods, and profits from mining precious metals, many new villages were set up, as well as fortified towns with their specialized craftsmen. The population increased both by natural means and by the advent of many colonists from western countries, especially from the Rhine valley. So for many centuries the Czech and German speaking inhabitants of Bohemia and Moravia lived beside one another without any great problems, practically until the rise of modern nationalism.

With the prosperity of the kingdom the prestige of the Bohemian king also rose. Přemysl Ottakar II. (1253–1278) was called "the king of iron and gold" for his riches and his power. He was supported by a network of strong castles (such as Bezděz, Zvíkov, Písek), he enlarged the territory of the state by both conquests and skilful policy, and even aspired to the imperial crown. He paid for his personal ambition with his life in the battle of the Moravian Field, but the prestige of the Bohemian kingdom continued to rise in central Europe. Přemysl's son, Václav II. was also king of Poland, and he gained the Hungarian crown as well for his son, Václav III. When the Přemyslides of the spear-side died out with the murder of Václav III. the Bohemian state was the mightiest in central Europe. It had a whole system of strategically important castles and fortified towns, lucrative silver mines in Jihlava and Kutná Hora, and high quality coins, called the Prague groš, minted since 1300.

The Luxemburg dynasty began with the marriage of Princess Eliška of the Přemyslides to Prince John of Luxemburg (king 1310–1346). The most remarkable part was played in European politics by Charles IV. (1346–1378), Bohemian and Roman king, from 1355 Roman emperor. He had grown up at the French court and was unusually well educated for his time. He showed diplomatic talent and political foresight in his plans to link the fate of the Bohemian kingdom with the future of the House of Luxemburg. He took up the Přemyslide heritage and strengthened the power of the sovereign in a union of countries called the countries of the Bohemian crown. As a visible sign of this power he had a precious royal crown made, which was at the same time a holy reliquary. Today it is kept in a special treasury in the cathedral of St. Vitus in Prague Castle. He judiciously built the foundations of imperial power from the countries of the Bohemian crown, and from the city of Prague the capital of the empire. He enlarged Prague by the magnificently planned New Town of Prague, had the Prague bishopric promoted to an archbishopric, founded the first central European university there (1348) and supported great building activity, mainly by the Petr Parléř building works. From that time Prague still has such Gothic gems as, for instance, the St. Vitus cathedral and the Charles Bridge. Charles IV. also had Karlštejn castle, the most famous of the Bohemian castles, built as a place of safe-keeping for the imperial and royal crown jewels. He encouraged learning and art and gave priority to diplomacy over arms.

Prague contributed to the European Reformation as a centre of learning. Two Czech reformers, the university masters John Huss (1415) and Jerome of Prague (1416) were declared by the Church Council in Constance to be heretics and were burnt at the stake. The teachings of the reformers became very popular amongst the masses of the people. A chalice became the symbol of Huss's adherents – the Hussites – as a reminder of the Holy Communion in both kinds. In 1420 the Hussites founded the city of Tábor in southern Bohemia, and from there their divisions rode out against "the enemies of the chalice", led by their commanders, especially Jan Žižka. Between 1420 and 1431 the Hussites resisted five crusades that the Papal See summoned against the Czech "heretics". The wars between the Hussites and their enemies abroad and the Catholic lords at home lasted for many years and caused a great deal of damage. But the Hussites resisted the Reformation.

Thus it was that King George of Poděbrady (1458–1471) became the ruler of two kinds of people: Catholics and those belonging to the Reformed or Protestant church. This king sent his diplomatic messengers to all the rulers of the countries of Europe, to the end of the world as it was then known, to Cape Finisterre, with a proposal for a peaceful union against the Turkish danger. In his own country, devastated by wars, King George brought about order, the crafts and mining again enjoyed prosperity. Though the results of this boom only became evident during the reign of his successors, kings of the House of Jagellon. Buildings were then erected in the late Gothic style in Prague Castle, in Křivoklát and Kutná Hora.

From the beginning of the 16th century the Renaissance style began – rather late – to come into fashion, mainly in rebuilding castles as mansions and in new buildings. These were mainly put up by aristocrats who were gathering in big profits from their large estates, with their newly founded fishponds, their mills and breweries. In southern Bohemia there was the Rožmberk family (Český Krumlov), in eastern Bohemia the Pernštejns (Litomyšl), and other noble families too. The 16th century was a time of thriving crafts and trade, so the burghers' houses also underwent Renaissance rebuilding, during which the interiors as well as the facades were altered. In some towns whole rows of Renaissance houses have been preserved till today, for instance in Telč, Slavonice or Nové Město nad Metují.

From 1526 Bohemia and Moravia were part of the multi-national central European monarchy of the Austrian Habsburgs. The central offices and the rulers had their seats in Vienna, with the exception of the time of the Emperor Rudolph II. (1576–1612), who moved his seat to Prague and revived its significance as the political capital of the empire. Diplomatic messengers came here and, thanks to the emperor's personal hobbies and to important artists and scholars of his time, so too did astronomers (J. Kepler, Tycho de Brahe) and alchemists.

Disagreement grew between the Catholic king, striving to concentrate all the power in his own hands, and the Bohemian estates (noblemen and city representatives), and this came to a height in 1618. Then representatives of the nobles' and burghers' opposition literally threw the king's governors out of the window of Prague Castle. Elector Frederick of the Palatinate was then elected king. Then followed a conflict that was known as the Bohemian war, but it was really the beginning of a much more extensive conflict, the European Thirty Years' War. In the first stage, the Bohemian war, the Habsburgs were victorious. The army of Frederick of the Palatinate was defeated at the Battle of the White Mountain near Prague in 1620, and Emperor Ferdinand II. demonstrated his victory by the execution of 27 leading Czech politicians in the Old Town Square of Prague in 1621. In the following years, when the war spread to the greater part of Europe, an important part was played on central European battlefields by the ambitious general Albrecht of Valdštejn, who was finally murdered on the emperor's orders at Cheb in 1634. Historiography and literature have not paid so much attention to many people as they have to this warring adventurer and profiteer and his alleged treachery.

After the defeat of the Bohemian estates the Habsburg ruler set a harsh trend of recatholicization in the countries of the Bohemian crown, and many people of the evangelical church had to go into exile. Among them the outstanding philosopher and teacher Jan Amos Comenius.

The post-war mushrooming of building in the second half of the 17th century and the first half of the 18th was entirely in the spirit of the baroque style. Leading European builders worked on baroque churches, mansions and palaces, for instance C. Lurago, K. I. Dienzenhofer, G. B. Santini and others. Their buildings are decorated with the works of baroque sculptors and painters (such as F. M. Brokoff, P. Brandl), that we still admire today. The Charles Bridge and M. B. Braun's sculptures in Kuks are unique "out-door" baroque galleries. The interiors of the mansions not only fulfilled the aristocracy's exacting demands for luxury and comfort, but also for entertainment. From the mansion halls, theatres, music salons and chapels came music that, together with that played by school-teachers and amateur church musicians, created a Czech musical tradition. It was thanks to this tradition that Mozart felt that the people of Prague understood him so well. Later, in the era of civic societies, such world-famous musicians grew from it as Bedřich Smetana, Antonín Dvořák, Leoš Janáček and others.

Industrialization went ahead in Bohemia somewhat more rapidly than in the other parts of the Habsburg empire. And as the power of Bohemian capital grew, so too grew the efforts for national emancipation and state equality. Modern Czech society took shape culturally in the first half of the 19th century, and in the second half politically as well, and the shell of the old Habsburg dynasty began to be too tight for it. On the threshold of the First World War, in 1914, Bohemia and Moravia were the most highly industrialized parts of the Habsburg monarchy, but unfortunately they were also its arsenal. Munitions that sowed death on the battlefronts came from the militarized factories of such industrial cities as Plzeň and Brno. Many Czech soldiers refused to fight for the interests of the Austrian empire and went over to the legions on the side of the Entente. These legionaries, together with politicians in exile headed by Thomas G. Masaryk, contributed towards the formation of independent Czechoslovakia, one of the new states set up on the territory of the former Habsburg monarchy in the post-war division of Europe. In 1969 this state became a federation of two republics, of which the Czech Republic includes the historic countries of the Bohemian crown, that is Bohemia, Moravia and part of Silesia.

Geographers describing the Czech Lands in the 17th century stressed the fact that they were surrounded on all sides by mountain ranges, overgrown with impenetrable forests, that formed a natural barrier to all enemies. These Bohemian mountains do not attain a great height (the highest of them, Snow Mountain in the Giant Mountains is 1602 metres above sea level), and they have become rounded through the ages, with the exception of a few areas of later volcanic origin, mainly in the Bohemian Central Mountains. The well-marked tourist paths make mountain walking and skiing safe. Some of the hills have become national symbols and hold their place in legends: Říp, Blaník, Radhošť. The Kralický Sněžník range is called the roof of Europe, because it is the watershed of the Baltic, North and Black Seas.

People who like sports with a spice of risk and adventure climb the cliffs that in eastern and northern Bohemia form whole cliff towns with the most bizarre shapes (Pravčická brána). Others climb down into the abysses and caves in the karst regions. Eliška's cave in the best-known Moravian karst, was probably the first in the world to be lit by electric light (1880). The idea of frontiers being naturally protected by forests makes one smile a bit in this nuclear age, but all the same this wreath of wooded mountains is part of the country's wealth. Here are most of the Nature Reserves (the Giant Mountains national park and dozens of other reserves and protected areas) that cover almost 14 % of the territory of the Czech Republic. The protection of natural wealth has a long tradition in this country. The first Nature Reserve, the Žofín primeval forest in southern Bohemia, was declared as such in 1838. This state was one of the first in the world whose constitution included the protection of nature, but the hasty industrialization often did not respect the laws. Particularly in north-western Bohemia and the Ostrava region nature today is really sick, and great efforts are needed to put this right. Professionals are dealing with the protection of nature and also thousands of voluntary nature-lovers, amateur ornithologists, gamekeepers and fishermen. Threatened and exotic breeds of animals are kept in zoological gardens, of which Bohemia and Moravia have the densest network in the world (15 zoos).

For centuries man has been taking mineral wealth from the earth: even in the Middle Ages he sifted gold from the sand in the Otava river and exhausted the gold mines in Jílové near Prague and the silver mines in Jihlava and Kutná Hora. Uranium is no longer mined in Jáchymov, the seams of coal are diminishing. But beneficial mineral springs still flow from the earth. The most famous of the 34 Bohemian spas lie in north-west and west Bohemia. An enumeration of the people who have stayed in Karlovy Vary and Mariánské Lázně alone for the sake of their health and for the social life would really be a list of the famous names of European culture and politics, and of course of the rich. The international film festivals too have added to the world fame of Karlovy Vary.

Bohemia and Moravia consist of many diversified and varied parts. Not only are there natural formations, agricultural and industrial regions, but also specific cultural regions, with different types of folk architecture, dialects, traditional handicrafts with products made of pottery, wood and textiles and a living folklore. Moravia has always been richer in folklore traditions, especially the eastern part of it, where we can still find ceremonial folk costumes, folk buildings with their traditional decorations and the noisy fun of annual customs (Carneval masked processions, the King's Ride etc.) In Strážnice, where there is an important out-door museum of folk architecture, with south-east Moravian villages, a well-known international folksong and dance festival is held every year.

Its hard to describe something that everyone must experience for themselves. For instance the atmosphere of a village in the south Bohemian Marshes, with the colourful facades of the farmhouses, built in farm baroque style, with a veil of mist over the surrounding meadows, mirrored in the still waters of the spacious fishponds. The atmosphere of a landscape that the poet has called "contemplative". Or again the restlessness and excitement amid the bizarre hills of the windy Bohemian Central Mountains, the harmony of the natural and man-made beauties of the region known as the Bohemian Paradise, the centuries-long stillness of the Šumava forests, the poles bristling in the vineyards under the burning south Moravian sun or the cacophony of the sheeps' bells in the Wallachian foothills of the Beskydy Mountains.

It is no chance that the national anthem of this country is Where Is My Home, dating from 1834, the time of the Czech national revival, when the modern Czech nation was searching for its identity. This song, unlike other anthems, does not sing of strength and power, but of running rivers, rustling forests and flowering orchards. It is not easy to live in the heart of Europe, the aim, since time immemorial, of usurpers and conquerors at the heads of their armies. Few countries of the world are sown with so many memorials to violence and needless deaths as are Bohemia and Moravia. They are scattered amongst those meadows, forests and fields as a memento for the future.

PRAG, BURG

PRAGUE, THE CASTLE

1

Die Prager Burg ist Sitz des Staatspräsidenten und Schauplatz der wichtigsten Staatsakte. Ein ganzes Jahrtausend hat an ihrem faszinierenden Panorama mitgestaltet. Auf romanischen Fundamenten haben die böhmischen Könige von der Gotik bis zum Barock ihre Paläste gebaut. Die geschlossene Baufront geht erst auf den Umbau aus theresianischer Zeit zurück.

Prague Castle is the seat of the President of the Republic and the scene of the most imortant state ceremonies. Its remarkable panorama has been formed over a thousand years. The Bohemian kings built their palace on romanesque foundations in Gothic and later baroque styles. The various buildings were joined into a single connected line by rebuilding in the time of the empress Maria Theresa.

PRAG, KARLSBRÜCKE

PRAGUE, CHARLES BRIDGE

2

Die Prager Brücken sind fünfzehn an der Zahl, doch keine zweite kommt der ältesten, auf Geheiß Karls des IV. nach 1357 von der Bauhütte Peter Parlers im gotischen Stil errichteten Brücke gleich. In den Jahren 1683–1714 erhielten hier dreißig Barockskulpturen ihren Platz.

There are fifteen Prague bridges, but none of them equals this oldest one, built by the Petr Parléř works in Gothic style after 1357 at the order of Charles IV. The bridge was decorated with thirty baroque statues in the years 1683––1714.

PRAG, ALTSTÄDTER RING

Dieser einst geschäftigste von allen Prager Marktplätzen wurde zum Zeugen bedeutender Ereignisse der böhmischen Geschichte. Er erlebte Königskrönungen, zu denen aus den Brunnen Wein floß, aber auch das Grauen einflößende Schauspiel von Exekutionen. Vor dem Rathaus mit der Uhr sind 1621 die 27 Anführer des Ständeaufstands gegen Habsburg hingerichtet worden.

3

PRAGUE, THE OLD TOWN SQUARE

Once the liveliest of Prague's market-places, this square has witnessed the most important events of Czech history. It has seen the coronation ceremonies of kings, when wine flowed from the fountains, but also the sad sights of executions. In 1621 the 27 leaders of the anti-Habsburg rising of the Estates were beheaded in front of the Town Hall with its horloge.

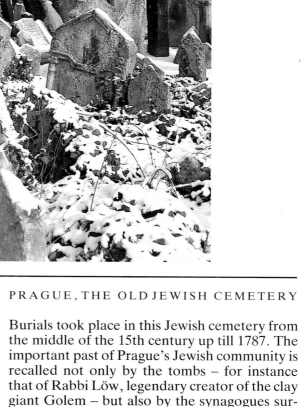

Auf diesem jüdischen Friedhof wurde von der Mitte des 15. Jahrhunderts bis zum Jahr 1787 bestattet. Nicht nur seine Grabmäler gemahnen an die gewichtige Vergangenheit der Prager Judengemeinde – etwa das des Rabbi Löw, der Sage nach Schöpfer des tönernen Golem, sondern auch die Synagogen in seiner Nachbarschaft.

Burials took place in this Jewish cemetery from the middle of the 15th century up till 1787. The important past of Prague's Jewish community is recalled not only by the tombs – for instance that of Rabbi Löw, legendary creator of the clay giant Golem – but also by the synagogues surrounding the cemetery.

PRAG, BERTRAMKA

PRAGUE, BERTRAMKA

Heute ist die Bertramka von den Häuserzügen des Prager Viertels Smíchov eingeschlossen. Als Mozart hier zu Gast bei den Eheleute Dušek weilte und komponierte, war sie ein beschaulicher Landsitz. Seinen letzten Besuch hat Mozart ihr in den Tagen der Uraufführung seines Don Giovanni im Jahr 1791 abgestattet.

Today Betramka stands in the midst of the Prague quarter of Smíchov. At the time when Mr. and Mrs. Dušek lived there and Mozart composed there, it was a quiet country house. Mozart last visited it at the time of the first performance of Don Giovanni in 1791.

SCHLOSS LÁNY

Das Schloß Lány wurde 1921 vom Architekten J. Plečnik als Sommersitz des Staatspräsidenten umgebaut. Hier finden auch wichtige Staatsbesuche und Zusammenkünfte auf diplomatischer Ebene statt. Auf dem hiesigen Friedhof ruht T. G. Masaryk, der erste Präsident der Tschechoslowakei.

LÁNY MANSION

6

In 1921 the architect J. Plečnik adapted the mansion in Lány as the summer seat of the President of the Republic. Important state visits and diplomatic meetings sometimes take place here. The first president of Czechoslovakia, T. G. Masaryk, is buried in the local graveyard.

7   BURG KARLSTEIN

KARLŠTEJN CASTLE

Die Burg Karlstein ließ Kaiser Karl IV. in den Jahren 1348–1355 als Festung und Schatzkammer für die kaiserlichen und königlichen Krönungsinsignien erbauen. Die Heiligkreuzkapelle mit den Gemälden von Meister Theodorich gehört zu den kostbarsten gotischen Baudenkmälern der Welt.

The emperor Charles IV. had Karlštejn castle built in 1348–1355 as a fortress and treasury for the keeping of the imperial and royal coronation jewels. The Chapel of the Holy Rood with its gallery of pictures by Master Theodoric is one of the most valuable Gothic memorials in the world.

SCHLOSS KONOPIŠTĚ

Obgleich die Geschichte des Schlosses ins 14. Jahrhundert zurückreicht, hat erst der 1914 in Sarajevo ermordete österreichische Thronfolger Franz Ferdinand d'Este für seine Berühmtheit und heutige Gestalt gesorgt. Hier führte er am Vorabend des 1. Weltkriegs Geheimverhandlungen mit dem deutschen Kaiser Wilhelm II.

KONOPIŠTĚ CASTLE

Even though the history of the castle goes back as far as the 14th century, its world renown and present form are only thanks to the successor to the Austrian throne, Francis Ferdinand d'Este, murdered in 1914 in Sarajevo. On the eve of the First World War he held secret talks here with the German emperor Wilhelm II.

9   BURG KŘIVOKLÁT (PÜRGLITZ)   KŘIVOKLÁT CASTLE

Eine kleine Burg inmitten der tiefen königlichen Forste bot den Gefolgschaften des Herrschers bei Jagden Zuflucht. Der Kern der heutigen Burg stammt aus dem 13. Jahrhundert, nach 1487 wurde sie aufwendig im Stil der Spätgotik um- und ausgebaut.

A little hunting castle in the midst of deep royal woods afforded shelter for the courtiers of kings since the 11th century. The core of the present castle dates from 13th century, after 1487 it was rebuilt more grandly in late Gothic style.

ŘÍP, ST. GEORGSROTUNDE

Aus der fruchtbaren Elbniederung ragt der Berg Říp 459 m ü. M. hoch auf. Die romanische Rotunde des hl. Georg auf seinem Gipfel war seit dem 11. Jahrhundert ein Wallfahrtsziel. Der Sage nach soll der mythische Urvater Čech von diesem Ort aud das umliegende Land als Heimstatt für seinen Stamm der Tschechen ausersehen haben.

The hill called Říp rises from the fertile lowlands around the Elbe to a height of 459 metres above sea level. The romanesque Rotunda of St. George on its summit has been a place of pilgrimage since the 11th century. Legend relates that this was the place where the mythical Forefather Čech chose the surrounding land as a home for his tribe of Czechs.

11   BURG BEZDĚZ (BÖSIG)

BEZDĚZ CASTLE

Diese strategisch bedeutsame und unzugängliche Burg haben die Přemyslidenkönige im 13. Jahrhundert errichtet. Bis zu den Hussitenkriegen war sie einer der Pfeiler königlicher Macht. Als Knabe war hier der spätere König Wenzel II. eingekerkert.

This strategically important castle, so hard of access, was built by the Přemyslide kings in the 13th century, and was one of the strongholds of royal power until the Hussite wars. King Wenceslas II. was imprisoned here as a child.

SCHLOSS FRÝDLANT (FRIEDLAND)

Seine Renaissancegestalt erhielt das Schloß in den Jahren 1580–1590 nach Plänen von M. Spazzio. Der berühmteste Herr von Schloß und umliegenden Landbesitz war der General Albrecht von Wallenstein, nachdem er den Titel eines Herzogs von Friedland erlangt hatte.

FRÝDLANT MANSION

A project by M. Spazzio gave this mansion its Renaissance form in 1580–1590. The most famous owner of the mansion and the whole estate was General Albrecht of Valdštejn, who won the title of Duke of Frýdlant.

DAS BÖHMISCHE MITTELGEBIRGE

Die charakteristichen Kegel, solitären Kuppen und Höhenrücken des Böhmischen Mittelgebirges sind durch Vulkantätigkeit im Tertiär entstanden. Über der malerischen Landschaft thront als höchste Erhebung der Berg Mileŝovka (837 m ü. M.)

THE BOHEMIAN CENTRAL MOUNTAINS

The characteristic cones, solitary hills and ridges of the Bohemian Central Mountains originated from volcanic activity in the Tertiary period. The picturesque landscape is dominated by the highest mountain, Mileŝovka (837 metres above sea level).

14   PRAVČICER TOR

PRAVČICKÁ GATE

Eine einzigartige, von der Natur geschaffene Felsbrücke, 25 m lang und 21 m hoch, durch Wind- und Wassererosion aus Sandstein modelliert. Sie erhebt sich über das Landschaftschutzgebiet Elbsandsteingebirge in Nordböhmen.

This is a unique natural gate or bridge 25 metres long and 21 metres high. It originated through the effects of water and wind on the sandstone cliff. It towers over the protected area of Elbe sandstone in northern Bohemia.

KRKONOŠE (RIESENGEBIRGE)

KRKONOŠE (THE GIANT MOUNTAINS)

Das Riesengebirge an der tschechisch-polni-schen Grenze mit der Schneekoppe als höch-stem Berg ist das höchste Gebirge in der Tsche-chischen Republik und ein mittlerweile über-laufenes Wintersport- und Wandergebiet. Zum Schutz der hiesigen Natur ist der Nationalpark Riesengebirge da.

The Giant Mountains on the Czech-Polish fron-tier, with their highest hill, Snow Mountain (1602 metres above sea level), are the highest mountain range in the Czech Republic and a favourite place for winter sports and hiking. The Krkonoše national park, which is a nature reserve, protects its flora and fauna.

KARLOVY VARY, JELENÍ SKOK
(KARLSBAD, HIRSCHSPRUNG)
Das bekannteste böhmische Heilbad hat
nicht nur die heißeste Mineralquelle, den
Sprudel mit seinen 72,3°C, sondern auch
eine herrliche Umgebung und ein reiches
Angebot an Kultur und Geselligkeit. Im
14. Jahrhundert hat Karl IV. dieser Ansie-
dlung das Stadtrecht erteilt. Erholung und
Gesundheit haben hier unter anderen der
Zar Peter der Große, L. van Beethoven,
J. W. Goethe und K. M. Weber gesucht.

16   KARLOVY VARY, THE VIEW
FROM THE STAG'S LEAP
This best known of the Bohemian spas not
only has the hottest mineral spring, the
Geyser (72.3°C.), but beautiful surroun-
dings and a busy social life. In the 14th
century Charles IV. promoted it to a
township. Among others to have sought
rest and health here are Czar Peter the
Great, Beethoven, Goethe and Weber.

MARIÁNSKÉ LÁZNĚ
(MARIENBAD), KOLONNADE
Entzückend an Marienbad ist der einheitliche
klassizistische Baustil der meisten Häuser und
Pavillons vom ausgehenden 19. Jahrhundert.
Hier werden Erkrankungen von Atemwegen,
Nieren und Bewegungsapparat behandelt.
J. W. v. Goethe, H. Ibsen, F. Chopin und
andere Größen haben hier geweilt.

MARIÁNSKÉ LÁZNĚ,
THE COLONNADE
Mariánské Lázně is charming in the unified clas-
sicist style of most of its buildings and pavilions,
built in the 19th century. Diseases of the respi-
ratory tract, the kidneys and motory system are
treated here. Goethe, Ibsen and Chopin are
among the famous people who have stayed
here.

CHEB (EGER), MARKPLATZ

CHEB, THE SQUARE

Das Stöckel (Špalíček) auf dem Markplatz von Eger in seiner typischen bodenständigen Fachwerkbauweise stand schon 1237 hier. Die Kaiserpfalz Eger und nachmalige Grenzstadt des Königreichs Böhmen hat eine ganze Reihe wichtiger historischer Ereignisse erlebt. Anno 1634 fiel hier in ihren Mauern Albrecht von Wallenstein durch Mörderhand.

The building called Špalíček (the little log), with its half-timbered architecture so typical of this region, already stood in the square in Cheb in 1237. The imperial fortress of Cheb, later a frontier town of the Bohemian kingdom, experienced many important historical events. In 1634 Albrecht of Valdštejn was murdered here.

PLZEŇ (PILSEN),
BÜRGERBRÄU
Der Pilsener Brügerbräu ist 1842
gegründet worden, doch geht die
Brautradition auf viel ältere Zeiten
zurück, wie das einzigartige Braue-
reimuseum verrät. Die Schutzmarke
Prazdroj – Urquell hat sich dank tra-
ditioneller Rezepturen, hochwerti-
gem Hopfen und ausgezeichneten
Brunnen auf der ganzen Welt
durchgesetzt.

PLZEŇ,
THE CITY BREWERY
The City Brewery in Plzeň was founded 1842, but the brewing tradition
here goes back much further, as can
be seen in the unique Brewery Museum. The trademark Prazdroj pe-
netrated all over the world thanks to
the traditional recipe, high quality
hops and even the good wells.

19

20 ŠUMAVA (BÖHMERWALD),
SCHWARZER SEE
Der größte (18,57 ha), tiefste (39,8 m) und am niedrigsten gelegene von fünf Gletscherseen auf der tschechischen Seite des Böhmerwalds oder Šumava. Seit 1911 Naturschutzgebiet.

THE ŠUMAVA MOUNTAINS,
BLACK LAKE
Black Lake is the biggest (18.57 hectares), the deepest (up to 39.8 metres) and the most low-lying of five glacial lakes on the Czech side of the Šumava Mountains. It has been a nature reserve since 1911.

ŠUMAVA (BÖHMERWALD),
BOUBÍN
Die Reste eines Bergurwalds mit überwiegend
Fichten, Tannen und Buchen erstrecken sich
über eine Fläche von 46,67 ha am Nordosthang
der Anhöhe Boubín (1362 m ü. M.). Hier
wurde von Menschenhand kein Eingriff mehr
vorgenommen, seit der Boubín 1858 als eins der
ersten Gebiete überhaupt unter Naturschutz
gestellt wurde.

THE ŠUMAVA MOUNTAINS,
BOUBÍN
The remains of a mountain primeval forest,
consisting mainly of fir-trees, spruces and bee-
ches, spreads over an area of 46.67 hectares on
the south-eastern slopes of Boubín height (1362
metres above sea level). It has been untouched
by human hand since 1858, when one of the
oldest nature reserves came into being here.

22 **SCHLOSS JINDŘICHŮV HRADEC (NEUHAUS)**

Die große Zeit der Stadt Jindřichův Hradec war das 16. Jahrhundert, als hier auf dem Schloß der Herren von Hradec wilde Lustbarkeiten und staatsmännische Beratungen abwechselten. In jener Zeit wurde das Schloß großzügig im Stil der Renaissance umgebaut und mit einer aufwendigen Ausstattung bedacht.

JINDŘICHŮV HRADEC MANSION

The town of Jindřichův Hradec enjoyed its period of fame in the 16th century, when the lords of Hradec alternately held lively festivities and diplomatic consultations at the mansion there. Then too the mansion was magnificently rebuilt in Renaissance style and given costly interiors.

BURG ČESKÝ KRUMLOV
(BÖHMISCH KRUMAU)

Der barocke Ballsaal mit den Malereien von J. Lederer aus dem Jahr 1748 ist ein wertvoller Beleg fürden Lebensstil der zeitgenössischen Aristokratie. Das vielfach umgebaute weitläufige Burggelände wurde der Reihe nach zur Residenz der Rosenberger, Eggenberger und Schwarzenberger.

ČESKÝ KRUMLOV CASTLE

The baroque hall for masked balls, decorated with paintings by J. Lederer from 1748 is a rare proof of the life style of the aristocracy of its time. The extensive compound of the castle, many times rebuilt, has successively been the residence of the Rožmberk, Eggenberg and Schwarzenberg families.

ČESKÉ BUDĚJOVICE
(BUDWEIS), MARKPLATZ
Die südböhmische Metropole Budweis wurde
für ihre alljährliche Landwirtschaftsausstellung, die Biermarke Budvar und den größten
Stadtbrunnen in Böhmen aus dem Jahr 1727 berühmt. 1832 nahm hier die erste Bahnlinie auf
dem europäischen Kontinent den Betrieb auf,
die Pferdebahn Budweis-Linz.

24 ČESKÉ BUDĚJOVICE,
THE SQUARE
The south Bohemian centre, České Budějovice
is famous for its annual agricultural exhibition,
its beer with the trademark Budvar and the biggest fountain in Bohemia, dating from 1727. In
1832 the first railway on the European continent
started running from here to Linz, drawn by
horses.

25 PLÁSTOVICE

Zu eigenwilliger Gestalt ist im vorigen Jahrhundert der sog. Bauernbarock im südböhmischen Moorland erblüht. Die Kunstfertigkeit der dörflichen Maurer fasziniert bis heute durch die Vielfalt ihres plastischen Dekors an den Giebeln von Bauernhäusern, Kornspeichern und gemauerten Torbögen.

PLÁSTOVICE

What is known as "farm baroque" achieved its own characteristic form last century in the south Bohemian Marshes. The art of the country masons still amazes one today, with its variety of plastic decorations on the facades of the farm houses, granaries and the arches of gateways in the estate walls.

FISCHTEICH ROŽMBERK

THE ROŽMBERK FISHPOND

Mit seiner Ausdehnung von 489 ha ist der um das Jahr 1584 angelegte Teich Rožmberk der größte Fischteich in Böhmen. Das südböhmische Teichsystem, das Werk meisterlicher Projektanten aus dem 16. Jahrhundert, fügt sich vollkommen in die Landschaft ein. Alljährlich werden hier mehrere tausend Tonnen Karpfen produziert.

Rožmberk, built around 1584, with its area of 489 hectares, is the biggest fishpond in Bohemia. The south Bohemian system of fishponds, the work of an outstanding 16th century projector, merges perfectly with the landscape. It produces thousands of tons of carp annually.

27 SCHLOSS HLUBOKÁ

HLUBOKÁ CASTLE

Fast die ganzen letzten drei Jahrhunderte befand sich Schloß Hluboká im Besitz der Schwarzenberger, die diese ihre Residenz in den Jahren 1841–1871 im romantisch-neogotische Stil umbauen ließen. Die Schätze im Schloßinneren wurden um die Sammlung der Südböhmischen Aleš-Galerie bereichert.

Hluboká has been the property of the Schwarzenberg family for almost three centuries, and in 1841–1871 they had it adapted as their residence in the romantic neo-Gothic style. The treasures in the interior of the castle have now been supplemented by the collection of the south Bohemian Aleš Gallery.

SCHLOSS ČERVENÁ LHOTA

ČERVENÁ LHOTA MANSION

Das malerische Renaissanceschlößchen steht auf einem Fels inmitten des Teichs an der Stelle einer älteren Wasserburg. Die Bezeichnung Červená (= rot) verdankt es seinem einstigen Ziegeldach, die rote Fassade datiert erst vom Anfang unseres Jahrhunderts. Dafür hat das Innere ein ursprüngliches Renaissance- und Frühbarock-Gepräge.

This picturesque Renaissance mansion stands on a rocky island in the midst of a lake on the site of an older water fortress. It originally got the name "červená" (red) from its brick roof, the red on the facade only dates from the beginning of this century. The interiors however are the original Renaissance and early baroque.

29   BURG ORLÍK

ORLÍK CASTLE

Orlík war seit 1802 Residenz der jüngeren, sog. Orlitzer Linie des Schwarzenberger Geschlechtes. Die ursprüngliche mittelalterliche Königsburg haben die neogotischen Umbauten B. Gruebers um die Mitte des 19. Jahrhunderts zu einem komfortablen Schloß mit reicher Innenausstattung werden lassen.

Since 1802 Orlík was the residence of the younger, so-called Orlík branch of the Schwarzenberg family. In the mid-19th century architect B. Grueber's rebuilding turned the originally medieval royal castle into a neo-Gothic comfortable mansion with richly furnished interiors.

BURG ZVÍKOV (KLINGENBERG)

ZVÍKOV CASTLE

Zvíkov, auch Königin unter den Burgen Böhmens genannt, ragte wie ein Adlerhorst über dem Zusammenfluß von Otava (Wotau) und Vltava (Moldau) auf. Der Stausee hat den Wasserspiegel allerding ganz beträchtlich gehoben. Die Burg wurde im 13. Jahrhundert erbaut und ist ein Symbol für Macht und Ruhm der letzten Přemysliden.

Zvíkov, known as the king of Bohemian castles, used to tower like an eagle's nest over the confluence of the rivers Otava and Vltava. Now, owing to the dam forming a reservoir, the level of the water is higher. The castle was built in the 13th century and is a symbol of the power and glory of the last of the Přemyslides.

TÁBOR, JAN-ŽIŽKA-PLATZ

TÁBOR, JAN ŽIŽKA SQUARE

Die radikalen Anhänger der hussitischen Lehre haben 1420 ihrer neu gegründeten Stadt den Namen des biblischen Bergs Tabor gegeben. Von dort sind sie in die Schlachten mit ihren Feinden gezogen. Heute steht die Stadt Tábor als ein Symbol der tschechischen Reformation.

The radical adherents of the teachings of John Huss gave their newly founded town the name of the biblical mountain Tabor in 1420. From here they rode out to battle against their enemies. Today the town of Tábor is one of the symbols of the Czech Reformation.

PÍSEK, BRÜCKE

PÍSEK, THE BRIDGE

Diese älteste in Böhmen erhaltene Steinbrücke entstand nach 1256, als hier an den Ufern der Wotau (Otava) Gold geschürft wurde. Die Brücke ermöglichte den mit ihren Waren auf dem sog. Goldenen Steig von Bayern nach Böhmen ziehenden Kaufleuten einen sicheren Flußübergang.

This oldest stone bridge preserved in Bohemia was built after 1256, when gold-washing flourished here in the river Otava. The bridge assured a safe passage across the river for merchants taking their goods along the "Golden Pathway" from Bavaria to Bohemia.

33   KUTNÁ HORA (KUTTENBERG),
ST. BARBARADOM

Das Gotteshaus der hl. Barbara zu Kuttenberg gehört mit zu den wertvollsten hoch- und spätgotischen Bauten in Böhmen. Seine Vollendung verdankt dieser der Schutzpatronin der Bergleute geweihte Dom der neuen Hochblüte von Silberbergbau und Münzprägerei gegen Ende des 15. Jahrhunderts.

KUTNÁ HORA,
ST. BARBORA'S CHURCH

The Church of St. Barbora in Kutná Hora is one of the most valuable high and late Gothic buildings in Bohemia. The completion of the church, consecrated to the patron saint of miners, enabled new prosperity for the silver mines and the minting of coins in Kutná Hora at the end of the 15th century.

SCHLOSS LITOMYŠL

Das Renaissanceschloß in Litomyšl hat G. Avostalis in den Jahren 1568–1581 für den bedeutenden Politiker Vratislav von Pernstein erbaut, die Fassade hat S. Vlach mit seinen Sgrafitti dekoriert. Mit der Geschichte des Schlosses im 19. Jahrhundert ist auch die Kindheit des Komponisten B. Smetana verknüpft, wie das Museum der tschechischen Musik dokumentiert.

The Renaissance castle in Litomyšl was built for the important politician Vratislav of Pernštejn in 1568–1581 by G. Avostalis, and the facade was decorated with graffiti by Š. Vlach. The childhood of the composer Bedřich Smetana is linked with the history of this castle in the 19th century, and he is commemorated in an exhibition in the Museum of Czech Music.

KUKS (KUX), SPITAL,
ALLEGORIE DES ZORNS
Nach Vorstellungen des Philosophen
und Edelmanns F. A. Spork entstand
in Kux während der Jahre 1694–1724
ein einzigartiger Barock-Komplex
aus Residenz, Bad, Hospital und Kir-
che. Zu dessen Dekor gehören auch
allegorische Skulpturen der menschlichen Tugenden und Laster aus der
Bildhauerwerkstatt M. B. Brauns.

35 KUKS, THE HOSPITAL,
ALLEGORY OF ANGER
A unique baroque compound, inclu-
ding a residence, baths, a hospital and
a church, was built in Kuks in 1694–
–1724, according to the idea of the no-
bleman and philosopher F. A. Špork.
Part of its decoration consists of alle-
gorical statues of the human virtues
and vices from M. B. Braun's workshop.

BRNO (BRÜNN),
BURG SPIELBERG
Die mittelalterliche Burg Spielberg, die natur-
gegebene Dominante der Stadt Brünn, war im
19. Jahrhundert mit ihren Kasematten als
„Vielvölkergefängnis" berüchtigt. Hier waren
französische Revolutionäre, italienische Carbonari, polnische Aufständische und auch tschechische Oppositionelle der Habsburger Monarchie eingekerkert.

BRNO,
ŠPILBERK CASTLE
The medieval castle of Špilberk, a natural domi-
nant of the city of Brno, became infamous in the
19th century, with its fortress cells, and was
known as "the dungeon of the nations". The
people imprisoned there included French revo-
lutionaries, Italian carbonari, Polish rebels and
Czech opponents of the Habsburg monarchy.

37 BRNO (BRÜNN),
    KRAUTMARKT
Zur mährischen Metropole schwang sich Brünn
1641 auf, als das Landgericht und die Verwaltung der Markgrafschaft von Olmütz hierher
verlegt wurden. Heute ist es das Kultur- und
Verwaltungszentrum Mährens und die zweitgrößte Stadt der Tschechischen Republik. Seit
1959 finden hier internationale Maschinenbaumessen statt.

BRNO,
CABBAGE MARKET
Brno became the Moravian capital in 1641,
when the Territorial Court and the administration of the Moravian Margravedom were
brought here from Olomouc. Today it is the cultural and administrative centre of Moravia and
the second largest city of the Czech Republic.
Since 1959 International Engineering Trade
Fairs have been held here.

SLAVKOV (AUSTERLITZ),
FRIEDENSMAL
In der Dreikaiserschlacht 1805 bei Austerlitz
trafen die Verbündeten östereichisch-russi-
schen Heere auf die französische Armee. Hier
haben 34 000 Mann den Sieg Napoleons mit
dem Leben bezahlt, ihre sterblichen Überreste
ruhen unter dem 1910–1911 errichteten Friedensmal.

SLAVKOV,
THE PEACE BARROW
In the battle of the three emperors at Slavkov
(Austerlitz) in 1805 the allied Austrian and Rus-
sian armies clashed with the French army. Some
34 thousand men paid with their lives for Napo-
leon's victory, and their remains lie beneath the
Peace Barrow, built in 1910–1911.

39 TELČ, MARKTPLATZ

TELČ, THE SQUARE

Die Bürgerhäuser von Telč haben nicht nur die mittelalterliche Anordnung innerhalb der Stadtmauern beibehalten, sondern auch den durchlaufenden Laubengang und ihre Renaissancefassaden. Der Brunnen und die Pestsäule von 1718 sorgen für die räumliche Durchgestaltung des Platzes.

The town houses in Telč have preserved not only their medieval disposition inside the city wall, which is rare, but also their arcade and Renaissance facades. That is why Telč is an important urban reservation. The Square contains a fountain and a plague column dating from 1718.

Das Westportal, genannt Porta coeli (Himmels-
pforte) der Klosterkirche, im Stil der französischen Gotik gestaltet, hat dem ganzen 1233 von
Königin Konstanzia, der Witwe des Königs Přemysl Otakar I. gegründeten Zisterzienserinnen-
kloster den Namen gegeben.

The western portal of the Porta coeli (Heavenly
Gate) convent church, in French Gothic style,
has given its name to the whole area of the convent for Cistercian nuns, founded in 1233 by
Queen Constance, widow of Přemysl Ottakar I.

Die Interieurs der Liechtensteinischen Residenz von Valtice atmen barocke Pracht. Ein Beispiel für eine außerordentlich stilreine Ausführung bietet die Schloßkapelle. Der Umbau des weitläufigen Schlosses nahm über ein Jahrhundert in Anspruch und wurde gegen Ende des 17. Jahrhunderts von D. Martinelli vollendet.

The baroque splendour of the Lichtenstein's residence in Valtice can be seen in the interior decoration. The family chapel is an example of this style in its purest form. The rebuilding of this spacious mansion took over a hundred years, and it was completed at the end of the 17th century by D. Martinelli.

TŘEBÍČ, BASILIKA

Die Klosterbasilika des hl. Prokopius in Třebíč ist um das Jahr 1260 von Steinmetzen einer Benediktiner-Ordensbauhütte errichtet worden. Ein Beispiel für einen Stilübergang, bei dem gotische Elemente in die romanische Bauweise eingedrungen sind. Erhalten sind ein bemerkenswertes achtjochiges Gewölbe sowie ursprüngliche Wandmalereien.

TŘEBÍČ, BASILICA 42

The monastery basilica of St. Prokop in Třebíč was built around 1260 by the stonemasons of the workshop of the Benedictine order. It is an example of a passing style when elements of Gothic were penetrating romanesque building. The remarkable eight-part arch and the original murals have been preserved.

43 SCHLOSS LEDNICE

LEDNICE MANSION

Die eichene Wendeltreppe in der Schloßbiblio-thek von Lednice ist eine wertvolle Schnitzar-beit und Kostprobe der höchst anspruchsvollen Interieurgestaltung nach dem neogotischen Umbau. Die zahlreichen und großzügig ange-gangenen Umbauten seit Ende des 17. Jahrhun-derts demonstrierten das wahrhaft fürstliche Gepränge der Lichtensteiner.

The oak winding staircase in the library of Led-nice mansion is a rare piece of carving and an example of the high standard of the furnishing after the neo-Gothic alterations. The many large-scale rebuildings of the mansion from the end of the 17th to the middle of the 19th centu-ries demonstrated the princely power of the Lichtensteins.

SCHLOSS VRANOV (FRAIN)

Das Barockschloß Vranov der Grafen von Althan haben führende Wiener Künstler jener Zeit nach Entwürfen von J. B. Fischer von Erlach an der Stelle einer alten Grenzburg an der Dyje (Thaya) gegen Ende des 17. Anfang des 18. Jahrhunderts erbaut.

VRANOV MANSION

The baroque mansion in Vranov was erected on the site of an ancient frontier guard castle above the river Dyje at the end of the 17th and beginning of the 18th centuries. The leading Viennese artists of the day built it for the Count of Althan according to plans by J. B. Fischer of Erlach.

45   VLČNOV, KÖNIGSRITT

VLČNOV, THE KINGS' RIDE

Unter den zahlreichen, vor allem in Südostmähren noch immer stark verwurzelten Bräuchen finden sich beim feierlichen Königsritt die meisten Zuschauer ein, da er als Volksfest zu Pfingsten stattfindet.

Of all the folk customs that have a specially firm tradition in south-eastern Moravia a spectators' favourite is the ceremonial Kings' Ride, which takes place as a folklore entertainment at Whitsun.

PETROV, WEINKELLER

PETROV, WINE CELLARS

Die Weinkeller aus dem 18. und 19. Jahrhundert heißen Plže und stehen unter Denkmalschutz. Weinkeller findet man im südmährischen Weinbaugebiet überall an den Rändern der Dörfer und Weinberge. Hier wird Wein gekeltert, vergoren, gelagert, auf Flaschen gezogen, doch sitzt man hier auch gern bei einem guten Tropfen beisammen.

This group of little wine cellars from the 18th and 19th centuries is called Plže (snails) and is officially protected. There are wine cellars scattered all over the edges of villages and vineyards in the whole south Moravian vine-growing region, and they are used for pressing the grapes, storing and bottling the wine, but for sitting over a glass too.

PÁLAVA

Das Landschaftschutzgebiet Pálava umfaßt die Pavlov-Höhen. Der weitäufige Kalksteinstock trägt eine Steppen- und Waldsteppenflora mit seltenen Tierarten. An den Hängen bei Dolní Vestonice (Unterwisternitz) haben Archäologen Wohnstätten vorgeschichtlicher Mammutjäger entdeckt.

PÁLAVA

The Pálava nature reserve covers the region of the Pavlov Heights. The extensive limestone cliff is grown with steppe and steppe-forest flora and is inhabited by rare animals. Archeologists discovered a primeval settlement of mammoth hunters on the slopes near Dolní Věstonice.

**OLOMOUC (OLMÜTZ),
RATHAUS**
Olmütz ist gleich nach Prag das
reichste städtische Denkmal-
schutzgebiet. Bis 1641 war es die
Hauptstadt Mährens, 1777 wurde
das hiesige Bistum zum Erzbi-
stum erhoben. Die Stadt ist heute
Sitz einer Universität und das
Zentrum eines sehr fruchtbaren
Landstrichs namens Haná.

48   **OLOMOUC,
THE TOWN HALL**
Olomouc is, after Prague, the
richest urban reservation. Until
1641 it was the capital of Moravia,
in 1777 the local bishopric was
promoted to an archbishopric.
Today the town is the site of a university and the centre of the fertile region called Haná.

ROŽNOV POD RADHOŠTĚM, FREILICHTMUSEUM

Das walachische Freilichtmuseum entstand 1924 als erstes seiner Art in Mitteleuropa. Auf seinem Gelände wurden hölzerne Bürgerhäuser des ausgehenden 18. Jahrhunderts, aber auch Dorfkaten aus dem ganzen Beskidenvorland, einer als Walachei bezeichneten Region aufgestellt.

ROŽNOV POD RADHOŠTĚM, OUTDOOR MUSEUM

The Wallachian outdoor museum originated in 1924 as the first of its kind in central Europe. Concentrated in its area there are half-timbered town houses from the 18th century and also village cottages, brought here from all over the foothills of the Beskydy mountains, from the region called Wallachia (Valašsko).

50 BESKYDY (BESKIDEN)

Das Landschaftschutzgebiet Beskiden an der Grenze Mährens mit der Slowakei nimmt eine Fläche von 1100 km² ein. Auf diesem Gelände befinden sich 17 Reservationen, die bekannteste ist der Tannen-Buchen-Urwald von Mionší.

THE BESKYDY MOUNTAINS

The protected area of the Beskydy, on the borders of Moravia and Slovakia, covers an area of 1100 square kilometres. There are 17 nature reserves there, the best known being the fir and beech primeval forest of Mionší.

Fotografien Dalibor Kusák
(Aufnahme Nummer 45 von Prof. Dr. Ludvík Baran, CSc.).
Auswahl und Text von Dr. Lydia Petráňová.
Übersetzung Norah Hronková (Englisch)
u. Jürgen Ostmeyer (Deutsch).
Umschlagentwurf und graphische Gestaltung
Karel Aubrecht.

Erschienen bei Panorama, Verlag und Editor 1992
in Prag als 4991. Publikation.
Verantwortliche Redakteure
Marianna Černá u. Jaroslav Havel.
Art-Redakteurin Věra Bětáková.
Technische Redakteurin Alena Suchánková.
72 Seiten, 50 Bilder in Farbe.
Gedruckt bei GRAFIATISK Děčín.
AB 7,81   VB 8,67   402-22-827

Erste Ausgabe.
11-014-92

Photographed by Dalibor Kusák
(except the photograph number 45,
which is by Professor Ludvík Baran, CSc.).
Planned and written by Dr. Lydia Petráňová.
Translated by Norah Hronková (into English)
and Jürgen Ostmeyer (into German).
Cover designed and made by
Karel Aubrecht.

Published by Panorama, publishers, in Prague
in 1992 as their 4991st publication.
Editors Marianna Černá and Jaroslav Havel.
Graphic editor Věra Bětáková.
Technical editor Alena Suchánková.
72 pages, 50 coloured illustrations.
Printed by GRAFIATISK Děčín.
AA 7,81   VA 8,67   402-22-827

First edition.
11-014-92

50
Bilder Pictures
aus Böhmen from Bohemia
und Mähren and Moravia